BEETLE BAILEY

is another in the happy series of books based on one of the most famous comic strips in the country. Its hero is America's favorite — and most reluctant — GI.

Here's a big handful of laughs (certainly one a page) by Mort Walker, a great professional cartoonist, concerning the most unprofessional soldier who ever hit the army!

Beetle Bailey Books

beetle bailey®

by MORT WALKER

CHARTER BOOKS, NEW YORK

BEETLE BAILEY

A Charter Book/published by arrangement with
King Feature Syndicate, Inc.

PRINTING HISTORY
Twelfth printing/June 1985

ISBN: 0-441-05258-4

Charter Books are published by The Berkley Publishing Group,
200 Madison Avenue, New York, New York 10016.
PRINTED IN THE UNITED STATES OF AMERICA

SOME OF THE GANG AT CAMP SWAMPY

KILLER DILLER

SGT. ORVILLE SNORKEL

ZERO

LT. SONNY FUZZ

COOKIE

PLATO

CAPT. SAM SCABBARD

GEN. AMOS. T. HALFTRACK

CHAPLAIN STANEGLASS

3-2

3-31

WHEN'S HIS FURLOUGH GOING TO BE OVER, SIR?

MORT WALKER

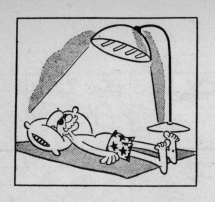

6-16

BUNNY, WHY DOES YOUR FATHER ALWAYS LOOK AT ME AND WALK AWAY SHAKING HIS HEAD?

OH, ER-- HE HAS SOMETHING BOTHERING HIM

IN HIS NECK?

ON THE COUCH !!!

MORT WALKER

12-19

I **LIKE** THIS SUGGESTION-BOX IDEA

SUGGESTI

MORT WALKER

6-21

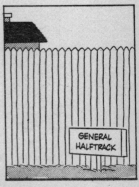

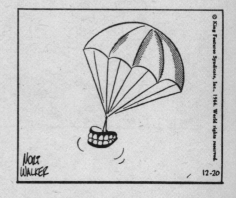

10-23

Mort Walker

© King Features Syndicate, Inc., 1962.

MEN, I WANT TO CONGRATULATE YOU ON GETTING TO YOUR POSTS SO SOON AFTER THE ALERT SOUNDED

9-3

THERE ARE ONLY A FEW SMALL THINGS I'D LIKE TO SEE CORRECTED

FIRST, THERE'S THE PEANUT BUTTER ON THE BAYONETS...

Mort WALKER

EVERYBODY GOES TO THE CHAPLAIN WITH THEIR PROBLEMS

FROM PRIVATES TO GENERALS -- HE ADVISES THEM ALL

CHAPLAIN'S OFFICE

8-1

AND YOU SHOULD SEE SOME OF THE PROBLEMS HE'S ASKED TO SOLVE

NEVER RAISE ON THE THIRD ROUND WITH TWO PAIR